The LAST **WORDS**

The LAST **WORDS**

David D M Osano

To order additional copies of this book, contact:
Xlibris Corporation
0-800-644-6988
www.xlibrispublishing.co.uk
Orders@xlibrispublishing.co.uk
301398

CONTENTS

For all that were
For all that are
And for all that will
I pride to know I have served with you

We will remember them . . . .

Dear Reader,

May I take this opportunity to say a thank you on behalf of the thousands of service personnel for your support and thoughts for those who we have lost and those who have sacrificed the most through injury in serving our country.

Help 4 Heroes as a charity was formed in 2007 to support those wounded in the service of our country all across the Armed Forces. The organisation relies on donations and volunteers to see to it that the wounded are supported be it through life experiences or providing essential equipment like wheel chairs to help aid mobility for those not able to walk anymore.

Having served with the British Army, I am proud to know that there is a lot of support out there to our wounded soldiers by individuals and organisations alike. I Support Help 4 Heroes for its wide network and for being able to identify those causes that directly benefit our wounded soldier. It achieves this by working with other service charities that directly support the wounded soldiers.

Help 4 Heroes will never be short of goodwill in its efforts but your support and commitment be it in donations or volunteering to run projects that help our wounded will always be highly valued. Your first step has been by acquiring a copy of this book as the author dedicates most of his earnings to Help 4 Heroes.

I hope that you will extend your support to all projects by this organisation to help our wounded soldiers. For more information visit *www.helpforheroes.org.uk* to see the incredible support being offered to our soldiers.

Thank you for your support.

David DM Osano

LAST WORDS

The silence that befalls after is unbearable
To know it is all happening and not know how
For all that we are trained for and learn over time
From the constant jolts of the sergeants commands
To the tasking demands of fighting for peace
The love I hold will never be shy
Even when pride and courage mask my fears
To know my comrades would as I would
For in one we became soldiers
Knowing not to give in nor give up
Knowing not to retreat nor surrender
From the unforgiving snow down Salisbury plains
To the dust ridden storms of the Far East
From the tamed enemy behind the wall
To the unmasking reality of life being lost
From the eloquence and gusto of the orders we make
To the loud but silent call to fight on
For in chaos all seems lost
To hear the word yet not be able to act
To want to be divine and if so heal your mate
To not want to be the one who bears the sad words
Words that would to the family be a relief
Not for the pride of what we have done
But knowing we were never alone
For those last words that we say every single night
Gone but never forgotten.

DESTITUTE

For the beloved in nature and creatures
Of a land so unforgiving yet shy of blemish
For the cries and sorrow that bellies its people
To know of the long lost sovereignty it held
I bemoan you for what you have become
So destitute and un inviting to few
Yet deep within the desire of want still alive
Of the children in innocent naivety walking to their death
Not knowing of the evil that is ploughed in their land
Of parents helpless in defence of family
For the pride of land remains daunted and ripe
So ripe that the explosives seize not to smell
The land so beautiful yet destitute in truth
For the smiles will never heal all that has been done
And anguish and pain is but from being destitute.

SAFFRON WALDEN

I beckon your history to come from age
To call upon the Romans and the Anglians
A tale of a town so quite in beauty
From the stone church by the Normans
To the elegance of the castle in time
And a priory of the abbey
Not many know of the pride you hold
So engraved that the years have unscathed you
The cottages that dot the streets
And the gentle smiles that greet all
You have become a true treasure
Known to few if not many
For those who know you stay not to leave
Never crowned for all that you are
But the names you held stretch back a far
Chipping Walden you were at one time
To see the good and bad come of age
From the civil war to prosperity
To be honoured by the likes of Cromwell
Or so be it you lost your flowers
To be replaced by malt and barley
You still held your head high
For to many you are the flower long lost
And if you are to lose any more
I beseech that you save the market in the square
And the turf maze in the park
If not only to smile again
For all those that yearn to discover all you are.

REEN

All alone, engulfed in loneliness
No one dares the face of a miser
So petty, yet harmonious in its emptiness
To be gracious the most for this plight and loneliness
That a day passes not before I dream of the name
Reen is the name that beckons my solitude.

Never knowing that all was set
To despair and pain for the uncalled happenings
But forget the ordeal, stand along
Lift your face above and look yonder
And hear of the plight, of a name befitting the miser
Reen is the name that beckons my solitude.

Waking by the cockcrow, to fetch a hoe
And in haste trace the way to the wilderness
That he dwells astray, from dawn to dusk
In an attempt of gathering food for the day
Just because no neighbour dares the name
Reen is the name that beckons my solitude.

How bore some it is, of the hellos of the day
To tolerate the plight and awes of the miser
For in hand I own the most, to call nothing in name
For I am proudly rich in my tattered attires
To speak of charity is doom to the village
Reen is the name that beckons my solitude.

This is not a chance to stretch a hand
For a beutide in maiden and gracious fortitudes
Thanks for the pre ordained act of celibacy I walk
For in solitude I am, to cherish the sorrow
Of missing the name that I so long for
Reen is the name that beckons my solitude.

Here I am, a man so deep in sorrow
To forsake even the masters will that dictate my misery
To see to it that his misery would pass by
Like a dream chariot that sojourns across the vast
To bring to me a life of magnificence
Reen is the name that beckons my solitude.

To save the neighbours of the daily misery
That my plight shall end and give its way
For tomorrow I live to hold in happiness
That the name will hold the beauty of its maiden
Like the zeal of the miser dreaming of fortunes
Reen is the name that beckons my solitude.

HELP

You know I exist yet you never say a word
I have lost all that I ever had in life to war
From beloved parents who to war I lost
To malnourished siblings always calling out to me
I sit and wonder what will become of me
The choices ever so small and demeaning
Bringing not a cloud of hope to my days
To be or not to be in terror I wonder
The lands will not let me plough for food
But terror is of late the only acceptable truth
I ask not for much in education
But religion is all that I am allowed
Despite the poison it perpetuates everyday
Blame seems to be the only agreeable truth
For in haste I seek to want to know
What makes you happy to not hear my cry?
How do I avoid being their servants
When all you do on sight is fight and bang
Fight, fight is a song through the night
Nights that in age was serene and beautiful
I know not of the years dragging by
Nor of the scorching winter and cold summers
I ask not for explosives or weapons in aid
But at least some water and food for them
To know in my desire they can afford comfort
Or so be it, it lasts not but a day
All I ask for is that in your pursuit
You stop only but to hear my cry for help.

LAZY PEOPLE

Across the valley, blessed rich plains
Is a home of the poor and blessed?
Poor for lacking money to feed
And blessed for having the day idling
It is no misery that they live long.

Comparative to the neighbours up stream
Of farms beaming with good seasons
Seasons that spells good harvest
But oh! It is no easy job tending the barn
To see their bellows growing in fat.

So goes the story of the two families
A family betrothed to poverty and misery
And another destined to flourishing grapes
Is it nature's way of discrimination?
Or is philosophy short of interpretation.

The rains have come to bless the land
A people happy, ready to plough
A people destitute, weary of floods
Not to mention the ever leaking roofs
Of wonders to see, that begets them all.

Is laziness a word or a taboo to shun?
To see land idling with no vegetation
Or is ignorance the art of our making
To curse the heavens for its rains
Pity to him who inhibits tradition.

After the rains, we welcome the sun
So once again we be like nomads
Gaping at the cloudless skies spreading aloft
With a million curses for its empty grace
That our people starve and succumb to death.

Time is paramount to non but a worker
Knowing he reasons and seasons of life
Of when to cultivate and harvest the land
And what to dispose of and save in time
Because by ignorance, we still live
To see another day of pure solitude.

FRIENDS

Good friends we hold, good friends we lose
So happens to all that are ready to share
Indeed, every person has a need
To talk of wants that keeps them all going
Beckoning on any prospect that comes their way
To pass by and give it reason to live
Do humanity cherish in vanity always
For all we are is but the vanity we adore
Holding one image yet divided in our destiny
Vast in animosity like the sand by the sea
Who by a swirl, get scattered till yonder
So perplexed by the absurd emotions of the sea
To get drifted to and forth by the waters
So are friends claiming to be united.

Like the proverbial building of the wall
So does the artistic making of a friend
It takes ages to make a friend
But a sudden jerk in emotions
Tumultuous in agony spares none
Because with it even the walls fall
A friend indeed, is likened to the stars
Who despite the ogling darkness of the daring night
Will strive to seat next to another
And bring forth a radiance of hope
Like the ambience of light twinkling across the sky
Pelting darkness with the worst of stings
For all this they achieve in unity
To stand and be called a constellation in war.

Betrayal is not only for the disciples in custom
For in them there was only fellowship
That enticing that they sojourn and save others
So reversible in its contempt that they did succeed
A common feature than a lepers wound
Betrayal is all we hold as the bond in us
Surmounting upon it names of grace
To talk of unfaithfulness where we err
To talk of selfishness when we fall below expectations
To talk of unreliability when we can never be sure
To talk of pride when we harbour in us jealousy
To talk of competition when we hide envy
But at the end of the day we still appreciate
Of how good it is to have a friend.

Even as the sun sets across the vast
We hold in esteem a new day in us
Of hope and redemption that we live not to err
To help us enjoin and share with friends
Hopes that are a more than the wish of a dream
Because in dreams we hold uncertainty of friends
To talk of nightmares when our friends betray us
I would rather that we take time
To weigh the laden of guilt that suits us
Deep down the darkened soul where we rarely visit
A soul that speaks not in truth by mouth
But of phrases and proverbs wrongly interpreted
Like to witness a friend weeping tears of joy
Yet at the same time in agony give crocodile tears
That in truth is what we are, friends in deed lest we betray.

IF I GO

If I go not to ever come back
To learn that all I had is but forsaken
To my mother and father in their uncertainty

Only to learn of my courage after all is lived for
To my daughters who in time would want my arm
As they take the challenge of their lives in time.

And to my sons who in haste will not stop
But to try and make me proud in being me
All calling and waiting to meet daddy from work.

Even when my wife grows to hate the door bell
And the solemn sounds of cars pulling in
For the dread of the words seldom said.

So strong she will not stand and sigh in defeat
But in repression fight not for me and my victory
But for the innocent loved ones left behind.

To tell them all is well that won't be well
To make them believe death when Santa is still a fairy
Will they stop and remember who I am?

Far be I to have travelled and fought in vain
For all my medals and salutations over the years
Will they walk past and be glad I am but no more?

NGULABYO

Magnificent scenery of beauty beheld
Of great hostility in natures accord
So is the street I call home
A Street full of learned learners
Of bustards who drink and spree
Damn the cheap stuff that erodes their dignity
Calling it 'stuff' for it is not worth a noun
How pitiful it is to talk of pity
Even the children enjoy this stuff
My street, wonderful street it is
You hold no destiny for us.

I cannot compare your irony
With any other worthwhile street
However damn it would be
Because everybody mugs in you
You boast of no muggers
For you never admit your faults
Folly from a comrade is no folly
A comrade to drink and spree
A comrade to pat and not console
I should know better to save the laments
To ask of your sanitation is but no ill
Though it is an act of utmost insanity
You have no mandate on you
Poor Street, wealthy with paupers.

The economy is bad, but the stuff is selling
You have no food for your needy children
Women toil all day long in the sun
To get some little cents for *matoke*
A delicacy to covet yet appeasing the emptiness
Greed being a pronoun of the city
Ngulabyo my street, when will you wake up

I fear your routes that snake its way
To walk along, with no light for security
But I wonder how ladies know it
They like the trained fishermen at night
Know in confidence where to bait a catch
They dress in aristocracy for the occasion
Like knights in gliding transparent armours
Waiting in patience for the patient night.

You are to me all but a nightmare
To pride in you is but an ugly obligation
With cars tweeting and hooting all the way
And motorcycles vroom and *proom* past
And bicycles *tingli, tingli, tingli* down the road
I cannot help but awe in wonder
For I was taught to look left and right
But in you, I dare not do that
For you have no accord in your rowdy street
Of unity, that in despair describes your state.

Ngulabyo my street, take no offence
That in utter faith I seek your leave
For my health is but history in you
Lest I drop dead and curse illness
Yet, all you give is the smoky air
And taps running with infested waters
I hope the day breaks well with you
That you afford at no cost the sound sleep
For all that is the misery that is there
But thanks *ngulabyo*, for you are my street.

MUKI SHOP

Round the corner, a minute presence
Like the Amazon down the forest
So you quench the people's wants
Small you are, but you stock all
Muki shop, a centre of need satisfaction.

Today I came for a cup of milk
Demanding so little but a stake for me
A ten shilling not spells poverty
Because with me I know no lunch
So, be well and offer me my needs
A cup of milk and a sachet of tea
A quarter sugar and a box of matches
Muki shop, a centre of need satisfaction.

The children in joy spare no song
Of praise and applause for a worthy shop
A place for sweets and biscuits in snack
What a jolly to watch them in the street
Playing *katolo* with *Muki's* bottle caps
A favour you give to a child to smile
Muki shop, a centre on need satisfaction.

Gracious God who heals the sick
From headache to stomach upsets
You stock the best, though dainty a prescription
What we call elementary prescription
To save a kicking soul from kicking off
And so to hell with the venoms
Of the vociferous mosquitoes roaming the night
In search of donors to have their blood
So at least natures resort to balance
But oops, do our children die for nature
Thanks for the insecticides you have
Muki shop, a centre of need satisfaction.

Surprised I was not, when you saved my ordeal
A brother in law at home, yet I am all but a pauper
Undecided on how to carry the dignity
Save for my empty pockets that spare not my ordeal
Though our favourite, of a helping hand
'*Deni*', they call it, '*kawaida*' we do it
Forgive our ignorance, not to read the walls
'*Hakuna deni leo*, no credits today
But the best is that in poverty we are ignorant
For by grace, I can feed my in law today
To pat him farewell on a full belly
A belly not fathoming and grumbling in rhythm
Making a hunger applause to none but all
Muki shop, a centre of need satisfaction.

Allow me the night, to go in peace
The sun is setting in, and I have to pat
To a house so gloomy and dull in joy
But before I leave, loving *muki*
Allow me a bottle of paraffin for my tin lamp
To give a ray and flame for the night
And a little more for my wick stove
I will see you when the month smiles
Blame it on me not, loving *muki*
For you understand my despair and needs
That I be not a miser round the village
Nor should I be the beggar seated daily by your shop
Muki shop, a centre of need satisfaction.

THE SERMON

A new day is here with us
To wind up the weekly hustles
To abide in spirituality and obey
The call for a free day of prayers
Not free to idle but to worship.

Serried in rhythm, like an ant trail
The roads all lead to the village church
The sun beckoning in its wake
Promising a rather polite sweaty day
Like pageants in a contest
So are the villagers in their best.

The Sabbath day is no ordinary day
Even the leper knows not his awe
To do the best and camouflage reality
They call this the Sunday best
Do we go for prayers or otherwise
But first the all so familiar hymn
To God is the glory for a new day.

Like the seraphins joining in a serenade
So does the choir chorus in unison
Doing all so perfunctionary duties
Of leading the congregation in solemnity
Unity losing accord, save for Pell mell of the people
Hymns sung causing even the peevish to wonder
Daring even the chirping birds to join in the wait
All wondering when the saviour will descend back.

Dispassionate as would be expected
Stretching his robe to and forth
A sign of an obedient disgruntled saint
But first, the Lord's Prayer is tantamount
Then the sermon follows on
Like a fall upon the great Nile
So is the daunting silence upon the church
On hearing of the great alien, tithes and offerings
A word not so welcome amongst all.

So, the going gets tough
A critical pugnacity on the people's pocket
God blesses only the hand that gives
So the bible says, not of the other side of the hand
That never in love gives to help but take away
The work of servants of God is on us
We feed the house of the lord
But if we can't, then the lord takes leave
As a father of this parish, I am for you
So the saint sings on to a flock so sleepy
Careful enough not condemn the paupers
Though in essence God helps those hardworking.

So before we take leave
The basket goes round calling for alms
Alms to the most rich of all
Both the poor and the rich alike
Wealth aside, it's time for giving
Blessed once more, is the hand that gives
Oh! What a sermon we had today.

TELL ME

Tell me of the love not the pride
Tell me of the longing not the gladness
Tell me of the smiles not the cries
Tell me of the gratitude and not the cost
Tell me you know and that you care
Tell me it's never been all but in vain
Tell me life is not but a sad number
Tell me you are sad for their loved ones
Tell me of the sorrow of your loss
Tell me of the debt in your smile
Tell me of the strength of your weak memory
Tell me you understand never to choose or pick
Tell me you admire and not abhor my profession
Tell me you would with vigour if you could
Tell me of the respect that will never be lost
Tell me in your comfort you still remember
Tell me not of shyness or of being scared for me
Tell me that with my family you will join hands
Tell me not of the bad but the good times too
Tell me to my face not for sympathy at my loss
Tell me of your courage as impish as it be
Tell me I am a soldier and be proud in saying it.

SOUTH AFRICA

South Africa, the home of my ancestors
Whatever happened to you, is not but folly
Blessed you were, flowing with honey
Of children embalming joy in them
Of a land naïve with ignorance
A land that knows not tainted progeny
I could live for but your roots.

Whatever we see today is not you
Profligate are the so called citizens
Not an insult I imply
But you know your real citizens
Talk not of Afrikaans and Boers
But the real citizens you cherish
Abide in your roots and give us hope.

So they came, in gusto and envy
Envy and intention of exploiting
Ravaging all your treasures
Like the wild beast out in the wilderness
But what do we get back
Indiscriminate and smacks and spanks
In pretence of bringing literacy to you
Literacy with bountiful boundaries.

They have all that we owned
Was nature so funky to hold resistance?
Upon the invaders from outside
Like ravens scavenging its wealth
All we have are distorted traditions
Empty and solemn gold mines
Where did all these treasures go?
And with frowzy ludicrous laws
Making us fugitives of our own land.

Seeking refuge like poultry in the open
Fearing to be torn and feasted upon
Can we hold hope for another day?
To see the foreigners go for good
To leave us with our ironic literacy
Literacy dispelling our traditions
Traditions that in unison hold us all.

South Africa my land, betrayal is no good
It's time to stand and bespoken
To tell of the good deeds we hold
To speak of literacy so appalling
To disdain naivety in our ignorance
And pinpoint injustices upon ourselves
This cometh not by freaking away
It takes arms on high to sojourn
And proclaim what is rightfully ours.

There is not a day no more to morrow
Rebellion is not for the literate
But fulminate dialogues are profound
Across the vast to the seas
It is a call of sentimental patriotism
Away with ignorant literacy
Bestowed on us by the foreigners
Away with the scavenging hands
That incites quail amongst us
South Africa my land, rise in glory.

GONE FOR NOW

I watched him go off to the unknown
I wanted to say all that my heart held
The time was never on my side
From the thank you that I never said
To I love you and always have
From please do take care
Not to mention come back to me is a must
He is gone for now to the unknown
And all I can do is look by as he boards
All the promises that I long to keep
And the trials I know will come
And the sad long days that are ahead
Never knowing the lonesome nights that await
Gone for now to the unknown he has.

FATHERS BLESSING

Listen small man, and listen carefully
It is your time to take leave and go
And please remember all that I say
The city is no hospital, to care for its people.

I cannot tell everything about the city
But I should trust you to be responsible
Go to the city and learn no traditions
Form the village you are, armed with nothing
And to the village you belong after the dwell.

Start preparing your belongings
And take road earlier, the journey is long
It will take days to have rest
But first know that strangers are many
Like a swan in the grassland
So will be your stay in the city.

Be manly and take control
I intend not your egoistic friend
But manly to resist the lust from within
The city has no girls like the village
All the good ones are present
So do have an open eye
To evade disguise of these city ladies,

To you they will beckon
Wanting for your money and belongings
You cannot guard yourself as you expect
But listen son, to have a worth, take heed
Come back and educate your siblings
As I said, the road is long and tiresome.

Dwell not among smokers if you smoke not
Nor should you company those in spree
Avoid their festivities, but uphold your youth
Small man, you go and give us hope
Hope to take courage and visit the city
Hesitate not, to be plunged in a dungeon
Seek your roots and comeback forth
To give me company in my last days,

Frail I may be, but I hold zeal
To see you mould into a strong man
One who by principle, Marries not
The incongruent ladies of the city
One who by corrupt ignorance forget!
And adopts the foreigners language
To speak with us not the tongue of us
Given unto us by our ancestors
Small man, go take the road.

Mould your destiny to a better future
Do not allow pride to chide by you
A foolish man chides in pride
At the expense of his soul
Forget not the catechist's call
Visit the parish and frequent it
To call upon divinity to spell your way
Distance yourself form the city cults
But say thanks for living another day.

Small man, though, listen again
Like the blind man's stalk, so is my heart
I part you but drift inside in me
To lose you to a foreign place
But I condemn you not to bring to me
A girl splendid and respectable to betroth
To honour my will and give me a grandchild
To covet not a life that is not mine
So go you, and start the road.

Last to mention lest I forget
Have my blessings and wishes with you
To be a man who admires many
And to the village enlighten our plight
By representing us to the great chief
Who so they say, speaketh not our tongue?
So go ye', and be blessed too.

FREEDOM

Welcome to my world
A world of vandalised freedom
In the name of independence
Independence to do all that I want
Not any that I plan for
So does my beloved country
A place I long for and cherish
A memoir of my last life
But still, I have no freedom.

In the quest for knowledge
I take my students through it all
The African ordeal in America
The benefits and demerits of slave trade
The advances dating from centuries back
Of a people in bondage of likeness
Of servitude progeny in despair
But that was then, this is how
Let's face the reality.

The administrators give me no leave
Watching every step I make
In the name of safeguarding integrity
So that I don't poison the young brains
With my inconsiderate talk on civics
Philosophy a damn spell for now
But education knowing no boundaries
Democracy, a polar bear across the Sahara.

Governments, big and small
Accept no democracy in its call
Proclaiming a bountiful independence
Where they choose what I read
They choose where I go

They choose where I spend my time
They choose whom I speak with
They choose the words I utter
And yet still speak of democracy.

Of frequent security raids at my home
Of discrimination on my family
Yet honoured I am, to be a citizen
A citizen to honour and abide by law
A law designed for but a selected few
A law recognising power and wealth
Of court sessions in the middle of the night
Court sessions with no audiences
And hang rooms flocking as the slaughterhouse
Not by animals but by the citizens of integrity
In the name of mutineers
Of treason charges to undermine authority
Mutinies that never were but words.

Speaking the mind being an offence
To be patriotic even in the wake of oppression
Betrayal by our leaders and elders
Running the country's affairs in a cloak room
No change forthcoming despite the concern
But hold the breathe, it's worth it
That was then, I still hold my hope
Of a real democracy to stand
To be justified in our call for rights
Rights to uphold and not sabotage
By democracy, we achieve independence.

ADE

Beautiful *Ade*, allow me your ear
Like a swirl across the valley
So comes the call of my heart
Sing in awe, a beauty so coveted
Ebony you are, shining like armour
Sweet *Ade*, come forth to me.

Like the shooting star in the dark sky
So are the memories of you on me
A moment silence of joy and not solemnity
Of harmony in the sweet smile you cast
Oh *Ade*, what white there is between your lips
Beckoning but the pleasant of touches.

Allow me the pride sweets *Ade*
Not to sing alone, but embrace your beauty
Forget the howling, lowing and bleating
You are but of most reminiscence silence
That casts a spell of joyful doom
Onto the birds in the wake of winter.

Beautiful *Ade*, allow me your hand
Your beauty so appealing
Like the hunters pride in betting a catch
So holds my memory of your beauty
Forgive the sun, to make you sweat
And the moon not to hide you in darkness.

Beautiful *Ade*
I hold no preserve
Allow me your hand in marriage
To betroth I do request
A magnificent beauty I covet
Give me hope, to cherish your love.

I will sing not so much, *Ade*
For I don't want to see you sleeping
I would rather it be in my arms
But it is never wise to welcome pride
I have another day *Ade*
Another day, to welcome you home.

DAUGHTERS

My daughter, listen to me
You have a long road to walk
Marriage is not but a bed of roses
It takes a wilful heart
To salvage the blossoms it hides

My daughter, I beseech you
Hold in you, the discipline you have
Do what is of you, and be obedient
Your husband is your long life friend
To love a friend is but a story
To walk with the friend is another.

Like the fish in the waters
So is your blessed marriage
You enjoy when you make happiness
If you dispel happiness, you invite crisis
So, be a good fish, to jolly in the best of times
And seek hide when the water falls.

Like a disco, so ids the sanctified marriage
Those inside admire going outside
And those outside want to go in
Be careful to do things right
To be a dancer who knows the time
Not to exhaust oneself before the dance is over.

Remember, beloved daughters
Men, can be so cowardly at times
A successful man, hold a woman by his side
There is no story of a man of failure
But trust yourself, to see the best of you
Learn to accommodate one another.

Like a voyage across the sea
Full of fuss amongst the crew men
Fighting and partying when times allow
But be careful to fuss but a little
And party the best you can
For you never know when the ship falls
Only then should you remember
To trace the root back home
From a man who dares your beauty.

AIDS

The unseen monster is here
Hideous like the thief in the night
Who knows his way even across the dark nights
So be watchful young men
Aids is here, and it is for real.

Avoid irresponsible behaviours
Be mature and decent in discipline
Not discipline to obey the teacher
But discipline to honour your body
Allow not the unseen monster enough time
To steal from you, your youthful days.

Abstinence is the best you have
No medicine cures this monster
Not even the herbalists can beat it
The wrath at which the monster kills
Each day summing unto thousands
Of beloved ones we lose
So young people, be on the watch.

Engage in activities to be busy
Distracting the monster
Amidst you
He is real and dwells amongst you
Waiting for the slightest haste to bite
Be deceived not by words of safety
There is no safe sex unless in marriage.

Hear not of safety tools, so you call them
Take control and mange your life
The monster surpasses these tools
Condoms are no protection against aids
So young men, be of wisdom

Do what is right at the right time
Create no sacrilege of matrimony
Wait until the time is come, for you to unite.

Be sure to have confidence
Know each other's medical status
Be free to discuss with one another
When it comes to aids, the unseen monster
There is non to fear other than your self
So, condemn irresponsible behaviours
Even from the trust worthiest friends.

Salvage the generation to come
Live not to create but a valley
With no youths to mould to adults
Because of falling to the unseen monster
Like a scarecrow, tell it on the face
No to sex, no to aids
And you will be sure to have tomorrow
To share and merry for a new day
But, remember, he watches you
Aids is real, it kills and destroys.

Breaking your immunity and dignity
Inviting unwanted ailments on you
What a shameful sight, to watch it strike
Of a youth full of vigour, succumb to illness
And then follows but the pall bearers
And the priests last words, cautious enough
Not to mention God salvaging your soul
He who lives a dirty life dies of shame
But in unison, we hesitate not to pat them
With silence that they rest in peace
Lest the monster hear our plight and strike.

CRY

Cry, so you say is good for you
When all that is near seem so dead
And all you know is no more
Cry, so you say is good for me

Cry, so you say is helpful to you
For the pain is silenced by the loud sobs
And the mind is numbed by tears down your face
Cry, so you say is helpful to me

Cry, so they say is acceptable by you
When I get laughed at for doing the same
For its weakness seldom revealed
Cry, so they say is acceptable by me

Cry, so I say is all I ever have
For to fight and cry is no shame
Even the might of the guns sometimes cry
Cry, so I say is all I will ever have.

MURONYO

Across the vast miles away
So is my village, *muronyo*
An Ideal place for a bored mind
A society full of humour yet no laughter
Of harmony in discarded inhabitants
Muronyo my village, I long for you.

Finely discreet, like a haven beneath
So are you, amidst magnificent hills
Oh. The *irima* that gives us pleasure
In the name of fine springs down the hill
Of cool waters that are the shepherds resort
The *irima* of *muronyo*, blessed be you.

Down the valley, flows the river
Like a stream up the Kilimanjaro
So is your bold stride of refreshment
Wonderful; sight of your work, *rowi*
A stream in the dry lands of *muronyo*
A land that abides with no wish
To downcast the farmers all seasons.

But forgive the spell, of dry land in you
Muronyo, how you surpass solemnity
Of a paupers clan, to give home to all
Thanks to the hot soup, *kamwaki*
That keeps the men alive
Alive in idleness and not in work
Kamwaki, the cheap stuff.

Muronyo, what humour you hold
Even to the young children
Who know no school and education
Save for the miles they would to go

But at last, there misses not a smile
Of children teemed in *ihenya*
Across the rugged terrains
To exercise but the tenacious youth.

Oh, how misgiving it is
To the village bar, *kerafu*
No one visits you save for strangers
Even *wathuri*, the dignified elders
All opt for *kamwaki*, the cheap stuff
Muronyo, you ordain even the lepers
From the hot *kamwaki* you provide.

But first, the magnificent sight
Of beauties from the stream
To watch and gaze with dignity
At the wonderful waists and boots
Of our maidens to be, *aritu*
The girls who know not when to flee
For suitors are never sleeping
To bring forth a hand in marriage
Muronyo, how treasured you are.

Forgive the freaks
Initiation is around the corner
The girls and the boys all alike
A stage to covet and rejoice
A welcome stint to adult hood
Muronyo, how respectable of you
To train your people dignity
I shall but never forget of you
Wonderful *muronyo*, my real home.

SWEET MOTHER

Sweet mother
Tell me how to thank you
Because I cannot but do it alone
You know you are all to me sweet
My sweet wonderful mother.

Let me begin by the origin
When I was nowhere around
You offered to bring me forth
Bearing the gory of all sake
To bring forth but a destitute.

Then the never ending love
Sweet mother, to nurse me through
From childhood to adulthood
By thy breasts am now grown
And still I adore your love.

Sweet mother
Allow me the grace and honour
To thank you for your helping hand
To give me hope when I was sick
To comfort me when I could not quiet
Ensuring the best of me as a child.

Sweet mother
To school I went, with you by me
From elementary to senior
Always giving me words of wisdom
Sweet mother, all I have is hope.

Sweet mother
Grown I might be, but I am yours
To desert not, a fountain spring
That brings joy onto my heart
Of a mother daring even death.

Sweet mother
Thank you the most, for your help
So it is true, to mothers' great hope
To give to hand that giveth only
Sweet mother, I will always love you.

IN-LAW

Brother in law, here me out
It has been long, seasons gone by
Ever since my beloved departed
A great solemn sorrow to all of us
But brother in law
Death knows no boundaries
Striking just but like pythons
Will I have to be destitute for long?
Provisions I do appreciate a lot
And my best is to say thank you
To see to it that your haven is kept
So I beseech you brother
My beloved brother in law
To mind of me not to be widowed
For a widow I am until tonight
Come forth not to aid my despair
Give me though hand of hope
Just as your departed would wish
I covet not, to a solitaire person
Not to create conflict of you
But please, brother in law
Hear me out, to part my loneliness
For in law I wrong not
That I hold to a wife long departed
Yet, all I see are those memories
That failleth to be memoirs
Lest I be gone in time
Of an in-law's plight.

STREET CHILDREN

Respectable, to honour thy destiny
To cherish thy reason for life
To mid and tend of thy offspring
What a misery to talk of street children
Of a town littered with destitute souls
Of children who know no love
Contented to be city dwellers
Yet out in the chill, are our fellows.

To save our children, is not but a task
Grown we are, for the plight of them
Them who have neither food nor bed
Not to mention clothing for decency
And vital of all, dwelling in ignorance
For there is not but education in street
Yes, of young ones sniffing glue
Of young ones in the blend of nature
Nature bluffing to be ever welcoming.

Our lovely children
Desperate in the street
Sick and feeble all day through
Forgiving but the sheepish smile
That casts but a solemn brotherhood
To beg from a stranger the least of a penny
But all we do is stride in haste in pride
Keeping our distance as with lepers
But they are our children.

Of a face so gentle and fairy
Hiding even the most awkward pain
To wait for a cold night in the street
With empty and growing bellies
To await a morning of orphaned hope
A morning not promising to save a chink
For even they sleep no sleep
With the cold biting into them
Like the deadliest of a desert sting
So is the pain in our beloved children
Poor children, meek to cruelty
Of a day full of gruff people
Assuming but their responsibilities.

LITTLE HUT

Little hut, little hut
Be offended not, to welcome me abode
To sneak through your little door
But condemn not my grotesque being
For in you I want to dine.

Small hut, small hut
A visitor I am, a stranger to you
To occupy but a fortune in space
Of your small room in gratitude
So grumble not small room.

Smoky hut, smoky hut
A compliment I hold for now
For you to show me your ventilation
To assure me of no suffocation
From the grisly smoke by the fireplace.

Smart hut, smart hut
Magnificent you are, standing aloft
To provide for each of your visitors
To welcome me and your fowls
But wait, how do we sleep in here.

Cosy hut, cosy hut
Gruesome you are, rebuking your cosiness
To allow the wind through your roof
And ensure but a sleepless night
To a coveted visitor who sleeps within.

Plump hut, plump hut
How poised you are to stand the hill
Like a tree thriving on a barren rock
To scare but he who dares your stand
And with zeal conceal your flaws.

Podgy hut, podgy hut
How many for you do you regard as many
To allow like a vault into you everything
Strangers and visitors all abode
Funky you are to lose your stature.

Young hut, young hut
How incredible of you to be resentful
Allowing in you even the fairest of brides
To start a life in your thatched roof
And sojourn on for years to come.

STOP

Make it stop and take it away
The noises and pain in my head
The screams and cries for help so quiet
The eyes before they take leave in freight
The body before in hope it gives in to loss
The chilly wind that is ever getting louder
The sun that scorches but fails to burn
The sweat that seeks to drop but only dangles
The arms that dip and drench of life
The feet that run and shuffle without haste
The heart that races and paces with somber harmony
The words so silent crying aloud to be heard
The call to stop that will never be loud in time
Make it stop, please make it all stop.

THE COMPUTER

A disgrace you are to but the foolish
To condemn you in the strongest breathe
With the very best of wishful regrets
Of a journey back in time
With no existence of your disgrace
Computer so they call you
To compromise our complacency.

Passing by a store yesterday
Downcast to merry in the city mood
I had to give in to an impish laugh
To hear a brethren comment of you
How wealthy it is to own television sets
But forgive, they were computer sets
How do you explain yourself to them.

To ridicule our customs and traditions
Of having to do things by ourselves
Going to the local grocer
He receives not in tidings my penny
But only commandeth the computer
Who stoically asks for more pennies.

Days are long gone
To hate to communicate yonder
A season distance to walk in the vast
But with you, I hear of Internet
To communicate to a brother yonder
True it is, but shroud my belief.

To give a comely resemblance
To one who admires fortune
And so they say, you also have pictures
Of different things round the vast world
Like from the sun onset and sunset
How do you travel, I still wonder.

Computer, damn name to call you
Tell me, for a coyly ignorance I have
When and what do you eat
And if that is less, where is your home
For I couldn't mind to betroth to you
As a maiden, my last bone daughter.

WOMAN

Discrimination is no apt word
To describe but the most resourceful
A creature begotten in disdain
A woman, to rebuke and lash at
Where are your claws to gnaw along
Because I pity you for being salient.

Woe to you, for being a woman
No generous word from men's lips
At a woman, a mother to all
Yet noble enough to breast feed them all
Woman, is time still far
To loiter and totter behind the shadows.

Woman, a disgruntled word to call
Your place to most is the kitchen
That being a betide upon you
Lest they forget, you fill their bellies
With the ordeal you go through
How grieved you are to be a woman.

Woman, how I bemoan you
To be condemned of all immorality
Like say that you mother all evil
And to every idle gentleman's word
No woman, no cry
How deceitful they are to you.

Woman, how I beseech you
To wake from your daunting sleep
And join the rest in condemning none
For if you speak, the idle stiffen
Because you know the meaning of life
Not idling around mimicking others.

But until then
It is wise to hear my cry
Woe to you for being a woman
To be but an element of relief
To a drunken husband home late at night
Who opts to be blatant the whole night.

SOLDIERS

Soldiers, soldiers
Off we go, tramp, tramp, tramp
To partake of orders by the colonel
To restore peace and harmony
To a people weary from wars
Fearing even peace itself
But first, you hear me out.

Soldiers, soldiers
How do you make peace in war?
Peacekeepers we are
But dared we are than the victims
To skive a bullet is but by grace
From young men in arms
Peacekeepers to make peace.

Soldiers, soldiers
Kill not unless it is necessary
So chants the colonel
Be friendly but watchful;
How do you befriend a tigress
Who is angered in war
But still, peacekeepers we are.

Soldiers, soldiers
Hear me out comrades
Break not until you are told so
Lest you fall prey to the enemy
Be no artistes of you skills
But like marionettes, a show of peace
For peacekeepers we are.

Soldiers, soldiers
Hear no armistice
But be very skilful to armistice
For the war has no rule
To kill and be killed
Is not but a local duel
For peacekeepers we are.

Soldiers, soldiers
Last though not all
Forget your families
For a glance in memory
Invites a stray bullet onto you
So on peacekeepers
Go out to make peace.

CITY DWELLERS

What a deceitful people
To dress decently as real gentlemen
Yet within hide burning flames of infidelity
Infidelity to even our beloved Akins
To cherish the ill smile of the city.

To welcome a stranger is but sin
For strangers are literal foes
Yet agog they are to rob the strangers
To ask for direction costs a penny
No token in a locked society.

Mugged to be is a normal life
But the law taking no course
To pardon by bribe the muggers
And acquit those offended because of bribes
So what a shame to take pride in the city.

To ask for water is more of a trespass
Part with a shilling for a cup of water
No free calls round the city
Going for a short call calls the pockets
How inconsiderate of nature at times.

Calling for an emergency
From the local police constable
Is but a wish hard achieved
For you fuel his car to run your wish
As if we make intentional accidents.

No office is an office
The obvious question being tantamount
Who are you and whom do you want
Courteous enough to fake a smile
On realising that you are a kin to the boss.

SILENCE

Sweet is the silence
That dispels solemnity
To all the solemn in spirit
To cherish silence
Is all about being silent.

So across the woods
Like a wind hissing by in rhythm
So is the silence that encumbers the woods
To cherish silence
Is all about being silent.

In the dock is a plea of guilt
But by the bang of the hammer
The accused gets innocently silent
To cherish silence
Is all about being silent.

So is spiritualism
To kneel and honour in silence
Yet applauding loudly by the soul
To cherish silence
Is all about being silent.

But pity to the newly wed
Who won't save any scathing insults
At a companion who resides in silence
To cherish silence
Is all about being silent.

Striding in solace
Along a street full of hooligans
To give in silence and spare solemnity
To cherish
Is all about being silent.

And to recall but the least
Silence is no York of happiness
For in silence, happiness gives in to sleep
To cherish silence
Is all about being silent.

FOR YOUR TOMORROW

For you tomorrow he sleeps in the cold not knowing what's next
For your tomorrow he knows not to have a meal lest he disappoints
For your tomorrow his life stops be it but for six months
For your tomorrow you are safe knowing he is out there
For your tomorrow he cries in sadness missing all those he loves
For your tomorrow he will never say I but we when called
For your tomorrow he gets called names unbefitting of his role
For your tomorrow he remains loyal to the ultimate sacrifice
For your tomorrow you walk past and run in haste
For your tomorrow he is all but given his today.

SHAMBA

It is time to toil
Every person in arms to the *shamba*
For there is not another alms
Even to the obvious paupers
To get in hand what the hand gives
Magnificent you are to justify life
According as a pleasantry food to all
But explain your humour to us all
Why we sweat all day long
Revelling curses to all but the soil
Who in haste give in not to our blade
For by a curse you turn the ground hard
At last, you are with good harvests
To fill our stores all day long
Before explaining why we sweat
For punitive you are to do so
To coy away from the birds who visit you
Seeking to ravage the plenty you hold
The plenty we call ours in a harvest
But what gain is it to you
To do all that year round and get no reward
Hope that you speak and tell us this
For a sweets *shamba* to me you are
And my sweat I save for your answer.

FRENCH MAN

Bonjour! Countryman
A good day we have
To say bonjour to our fellows
Hoping that it sounds well

I French, no English
English man so petty
We French do not get so petty
French man no coward.

To go to war and fight till end
Not like English who stand a far
To scare the enemy away
Like birds in the wheat farms.

But wait, salute English man
He does a lot for people
To teach even the most ignorant
And aid those dying of hunger.

I honour you English man
But still, I am French man
A hospitable being on earth
A French man shields no smile.

A French man lacks no gratitude
A French man says thank you
For French is thankful to all
Discriminating no one.

So bonjour to all
As comrades we speak
To cherish our country
And enjoy our language.

To be French is good
To speak French is better
To appreciate we know
Like the elegance, we hold.

From Paris to Venice
Abiding in the law
To honour the honourables
Like a monsieur in suit
So is the French man in smiles.

MIGHTY ONE

Hear my pleas, mighty one
I come humble and not to duel
I honour thee mighty one
To betray or blaspheme
Is but a mortal disgrace to me
But to thee mighty one
I bring honour and wishes
Wishes to live another day
Wishes to see us through safely
To provide to us rationally
To hold justice where it counts
To command that which is right
And give to us freedom to live
To sabotage any foes on us.

Oh mighty one, I call on thee
Allow me to talk of our little ones
Who in war are departed
For they were patriotic in its call
Bartered and tortured all way
Of our partners who freak
Always agonising when in memory
But mighty one, I trust thee
To step forth and quill all this
Like calm to a stormy night
I beseech thee mighty one
Not by mercy or grace
But remember thy servants
To stand with them in all this.

With all your might we hope
That you dare the daring enemy
To provide education to the young
To allow marriages when appropriate.
For you are a mighty one
And it is not in vain that I plea
To taint my pride and be sincere
And on my two knees
Beckon upon thy throne
Come forth and be with us
To be mighty so we maybe too
To dispel all our weaknesses
Oh mighty one I trust in you
And hope you hear our plea.

UNITED AFRICA

A noble race you are
To be bestowed with nature
All giving's and misgivings you hold
Africans unite.

To covet is great sin
Your magnificent and silent nights
To hear the owls scream and crickets cry
Africans unite.

But why Africa
Why all these daggers I hear
Why all the bloody hands
Africans unite.

What will you do Africa
Let's not consort with failures
To show an unfelt sorrow is an offence
Africans unite.

MY LORD

How now my lord
To be solemn in the early sun
Like a cricket knowing no light.

Oh my lord, how I beseech thee
That in my bosom you live
Like a guarded grape in its vine.

Where our desire is got without content
So that I pray thee to stay
Next to me and never to leave.

And by roses applaud in deed
Of a forfeited jocund I hold
There is comfort though yet assailable.

To save my palpable face
Of streams of tears a stream
To punish the deer with flood.

Oh my lord, hear thy will
To stake with thee by my side
The heath being so hot today.

As is seemeth in my plight to revolt
And jolts the sight of the grave
To choke my art, of my lord.

A damned doom to live through
So is the wish that is hideous in me
As two games, that clings together.

Things that sounds so fair indeed
Yet truthful in deceit it is
Speak then to me my lord.

Chide thee not in thy pride
Thee who neither begs nor fears not
Him who is no lesser than a soldier.

With gusto moaning the dark night
Oh my lord, woe my plight
Had I but went a sun earlier.

Having lived a gracious time
To know not a thing in mortality
That like the vine vault I be silent.

Drawing in present destroys it all
So it is my lord, that in my bosom
To tear it a jar and save the blood.

And reveal the will in me
For in love you be by my side
Oh my lord, hear my plight.

MY WILL

Mighty is the existence
Immortal in a mortal being
To command even the desperate
From within you speak
Finding it so inclined
To give no options to me
But by thy will slay my pride
Demeaning all that I cherish
Like the cistern of my lust
And the veil desires of my mind
Corruptible to spare me not
But deep down within
Perceivable to be though invisible
Like a valley in between
So swells my heartened bosoms
Like a legion you command
Even the worst of the worst
My lump limbs to caution
Just but to do thy will
Invisible being you are
Dictating all that I desire not
For you are indeed my will.

OF WITCHES

Cursed be thee, thick night
To stretch thy wicked blanket
What beast you are to devour
The beautiful reminiscence of day
So away with thee, thick knife
That my tender face sees not thy wrath
Bewitched is thee, to betray light
Meeting in thunder, lightning and rain
Daring a battle that is all lost
Charging ere the set of the sun.

To swarm upon land like famine
Who dares a good harvest in hand
So poor night, dammed be you
Disdaining fortune, with thy darkness
A haunting temple you are
To thank us by trouble making
Because hideous you are
To accommodate witches in the dark
Droned in lousy robes
That by stinking smiles they scare good.

To plan vendetta with an angel
They who merry in joyful troubles
Who allow no slip of the hour
Commanding with vengeance tonight
A night so unruly, yet we lay herein
Witches betrothed to hell they are
Acting with no empathy in them
Presenting us with weary disasters
Misfortunes tugged with fortune
Like a king commanding a besieged castle.

So you allow the black one to rule
And so allowing the witches to reign
Where your desire is got without content
So that by destruction dwelleth thee
Masquerading with joy in death
Fate being but a mirrors shot
To see witches embracing nudeness
Of an orgy witch howling in darkness
Calling forth to a companion in sleep
But save the dark for in peace it is.

To receive the light though in haste
For witches be dammed and dead
To languish in speaking all but wrath
That in prose you prophesy ill will
To set a blazing home in havoc
For by their words homes do part
Like fire between the lips
So are the words of witches in life
Making an irony of a man
To control the destiny of an immortal soul.

Witches be thee damned away from us
To shun he who in companion prides
Walking in hand with him that is a witch
For all that they are is not good
Always ready to swallow anything it meets
So they that partner in darkness be watchful
That you make not innocent partners with witches
Who are there best in the dark
For darkness holds no compliments
Save for the regrets that it brings forth in history.

NIGHT WITCHES

When shall we in oath unite
In thunder, lightning or hailstorms
To oath of our condemned acts
That by inheritance we be witch full
Salvaging no race in ambience
But strike in grace like lightening.

Take heart comrade
It is no reason to grumble in light
Thou know we meet in ordinance
That by the sun's humble sleep
We take leave from our slumber
Like bats do by dusk.

Ay! Comrades, do thou plan
To strike like in villains act
Of our brethrens in light
I giveth in, to start the epoch
Hoping non to be spared
Lest we forget to appease her majesty.

Speaketh you in light to applaud
That by grace, her majesty alloweth
That be we invisible even by lightening
To scheme our acts like in an abyss
So tantamount be it the goal.

Foolish people, knowing no darkness
To chide and dwell in dark lights
Bewitched they shall be in light
And by death be they in dark
For our battle is neither fair nor foul
To spare him that knows no darkness.

Cast upon them cold, to embrace in ill
That understanding they fail
Calling it all sort of intelligent names
Like fever, flu's, coughs, and shock
As seemeth by their plight of despair
To condemn themselves in unity.

Look what I have yonder afar the sky
Cometh in haste, sparing no sailor
He sky is beckoning with darkness
Off with our nightly sessions
To spare our tarts from lowering
That tonight we be not insane to sleep.

DARK LOVE

To my distant love, hidden by time
Though the distance dictates our role
But the heart carries our strong will
So we pray that we be not separated
By the ugly distance that is between.

For the best we have needs the will
That the distance breaketh not
For by love we travel in wishes
Big enough to outdo the dreams
But to you my love you are more.

All we deserve for in love it gives
Is not but the utter unity of lovers
But the sound beckoning of love
Them that mind not to play like kids
For in the woods they play at night.

Knowing not the presence of darkness
For the best of love is never specified
To dwell in light nor in darkness
Yet, the smiles are hidden lest they betray
Even the most ignorant in the deep night.

To savour the best until the priest adorns
For by the veil we walk in unity
And with love we run to our hideout
That the embers forever will keep burning
Never stopping until the sun goes down.

For in night we speak of sweet darkness
In addition, blind we be not to see the moon
But with zeal trace our way from the woods
For tonight is the greatest that we share
For love is always its best on every new day.

CLOUDY LOVE

Of love so tameable in smile
That I get to sing of thee in my sorrow
To see to it that a shed no tear
For my guilt is eating me
That I failed in my pledge to you
To see to it that in love I be yours
In good and in bad weather
Like the cloudy days when love is lonely
And the sunny days when love is outgoing
That it seeks to count sand by the sea
How is beg thy forgiveness today
That I live not to be a fugitive again
For I hurt in storm a soul so loving
Never considering the timing of the clouds
If love be so realistic to pardon
So cometh my plea to be forgiven
That I live to hold thy hands again
And hold the pleasure to smile along
That we surpass in unison the cloudy times
And walk the life full of love.

STREET FOLKS

Twinkled as it seems
you never miss the mysteries
of street full of diversity
one that in ethnicity has no name
for it is convenient in anonymity
like the stranger in the foreign land
so I talk of the street folks
them who in content like poverty
that they move around in harmony
filled with solitude and despair
that no one taunts the other
for street folks are friends
who in respect adore one another
but ever thought of the mess you make
to pack the walks that no space is left
for visitors deserve what is absent in you
dignity being a long gone ambition
for filth is all that is adorning you
hiding in grace your disgraceful beauty
street folks in poverty who hold no love

ADES

Ades is the fairy's name
of the maiden in honour
who seeks not in love to be loved
the plight of those in it being worthy
for ades knows the being and feelings
that calls for right time to extend in love
to see and watch from yonder as they dance
as the parade passes by along the street
enjoining in passion the bride to be
how I long to sing and sing
of this ebony's beautiful name
that it rises and sets as the sun
upon the very lonely soul I hide
for in reality it is too happy
to get to speak and whisper
a name so fairy to deserve more
in happiness and joy in love
but till then I seek to admit
that love never ended on the spring morning
for *Adembesa* was never fully spelt.

CINTHIAH

To talk of the tales that never died
that once in time we had in history
of a fairy in tale who to many was loved
that she bespoke of the will in love
summoning in humility the greatest of men
who in fantasy kill their strong ego
for the name and sight was too strong
that they miss and sputter the name in haste
the name so tough that in love to pronounce
cinthiah I was taught on several occasions
to forgive my err that I sing of it
lest I stumble and lose it all
thence I will in totality be dead
for even the name of the fairy will fall
cinthiah I sing beyond the clouds
she that beckons the wilful souls
striking in gusto there meek hearts
that they live to regret never winning
the love abound that the fairy offers
so am I to shun my strong and meek ego.

HURICANE KATRINA

What an awesome sight
To see the beauty in pain
Of a land so welcoming in life
Yet so down in happiness
Of kids dying of hunger
From a society that is rich
Death not from fate,
But rather from neglect
Neglect of a society united in grief
A society that knows not hope from its mentors
A society that has for a while been adamant in bliss
Yet Katrina in its rage thwarts it all
Sweeping away even the mightiest of monuments
What next to be expected from the horrible Katrina.

GLOUCESTER CATHEDRAL

Magnificent work of art
Is the tribute I hold for you
For you stand so tall in and elegant
Brisk enough to be noticed
Humble in beauty to be compared
For in you a history is written.

Of the souls that come in pain
And hearts that ache in grief
And minds that wander in solitude
You create to them the walls
Fortified enough to keep away ill will
Warm enough to disguise winter.

And yet still even in your sombre love
You try in vain to reach out to the mass
Who in love take pictures of you
For a post card you are to be cherished
How you long for them to be embracing
And share the love that you speaketh of in time.

I love the sound of the bell pitching the night
To silence the grumpy drunken folks
Who in guilt drink in haste to run away
For thy gong sound sirens in their ways
Lest they fail to be awakened in there drink
Partying all through the lonely dark nights.

In Gloucester you are a land mark to many
For poets and politicians all alike
Never stopping to look at your presence
Commanding a troop that knows not to fight
Should it only be memories we hold of thy fight in time?
Or should we rather be of courage and question thy neglect
For still your religious role is paramount
Lest the mass takes charge to flee
And adorn you only in tourism.

ELIM

Amazing grace and sweet are thy words
To be in awe rejoicing in sadness
Bringing together lost souls in Christ
How I love to be in thy company
That which takes away the solitude guilt
Of not being near the rejuvenation of our souls
Elim centre always a place of hope.

From the young who in smile stride past everyday
Never seeing the ego in you as you smile back
Telling of the sweet words that coin thy name
So treasured to them they forget to stop by
Lest they get caught in thy endearing love
So wonderful that forever you wish to be young
Elim centre always a place for growth.

Forget not the vows sang in happiness
Joy in words that we cherish to last with
To say I do under your roof is a longing wish
For with growth we learn the word
As we get ready to walk in two down the aisle
Lucky it' not so long to be worn out walking
Elim centre always a place of love.

With papas and mamas holding our hands
Admire the beauty of the smile spelt by years
Years of love and true fellowship
To know that there is only one best way in life
Having been there and done everything
Share the love is what our senior citizens teach
Elim centre always a place of worship.

Singing in tune to the beat of the drums
With the guitarist fiddling in sweetness
And the pianist swaying in rhythm
As the hymns carry in style the true beauty
Of being able to worship and praise
And the pastor ever so smiling
With knowledge of the presence of the spirit
Elim centre always a place forever home.

SORRY

Days seem to really fly in haste
In pursuit of the awaited happiness
Yet of course never looking back
For I know that I really did wrong
To walk by and never say hello
Does not mean I stopped
Wish I knew a better way to do so
But I just cannot find the will to do it

I long for the sweet days
When I could look into you and smile
And you would look back and blush
With the shyness filling your pretty eyes
I am really sorry I still miss all these
Knowing for sure it was my own err'
To walk away when you needed me
To play silly when I ought not to
To be of no feelings when deep down it was overflowing
No amount of words can do any better
For I don't even see you to get to say I am sorry

Days when like my mum I slept away
Under the loving watch that described you
To know when in pain I needed you
And when am empty you filled me in
Does not mean I forgot about all these
I do know but I cannot get the will
To be so pleasant to say I am sorry
Lest I drown in the tears that well my eyes
For to go in tears would make me ill
And that alone does you a lot of pain

I am really sorry for all that I have done
Just remember that I still love you
And really do appreciate all that you mean to me
For without you I seek way
Lost in the dark wild world.

Wish you luck in all you do
Hoping that with time the hate will heal
For it's not of love to bear hate
Lest I hate to know I still love you
But whatever time you make it
There will always be this lonesome feeling
Ever etching its mark from losing you
Ever so tameable to say sorry
Ever so warm top see you smile back
For in all we got the most of happiness
Just remember that all is true that was said.

SMILING BEAUTY

She never would know how precious she is
To smile and smile and light up my face
That I awaken in smiles at hers
For she is really all that I really want
Life to us will never be what it was
But rather a pleasant and fruitful one
For I get to sing of her beauty even as I snore
I hope I did not say I snore . . .
If she smiles then I snore
If she doesn't then she snores
For I know that she is fighting not to . . .
Not knowing that it's more beautiful when she tries not to.
I love her with all that I am
And want to be all that she wants
For I know that I am the luckiest so far
To get to see her smile even as she smiles in her sleep
What a face so pretty to ignore . . . .

If be Shakespeare and loathe my language
How I plea with thee that ye be my lady
That in sombre happiness I seek thy hand
Not to say marry me but more than that
For I know thee that see'th even in darkness
And causes darkness to stir the light . . .

I can be catty and sing like a bird
Or rather chat like a parrot
But even parrots when in love chat a lot
So if I be a parrot to say I love thee . . .
So be it my lady, I really do
Over and yonder my love calleth
That in spree it sobers up
To the demands of the drunken being
That which in ignorance says not

Walk by the soul and thy heart will follow
Never knew what that would mean
Hope that I do know it now . . . .
The very way that I did not know what a kiwi was
But in smiles my lady taught me what it was
Was it in fault that she did?
I hate to say know, coz still ill love her
She woops and smacks when I miss to miss
Yet she doddle's and fondles when I need to cuddle
What a lady in honour thou art to me
That I seek to be blessed and bless very few
For even the oldies never lived to be me.
Like the stray wind they came . . . .
And off they went just as the easterly clouds across the desert
Longing to bring rain to a land that longs not
I speak not to me self if I feel this . . . .
For my lady deserves more than just a smile
Lest, she mums and smiles no more . . .
How saddening that will be to my loving heart
For to make or break is not a choice and an option

If she reads this then she is really well
If she reads the next line then her throat is getting better
If she prints this then she knows I love her
If she does print it then I still love her . . .

THE RIVER

It is yet another rainy season
To see the river flow with joy
Bringing with it all that it can carry
So to speak, blessed are them
Who by the river, have a livelihood
To receive of the good and bad
Of the fertile land and dirt
Of carcasses of animals washed away
But then, that is the river.

Up the hills and down the valleys
A ray of hope to those in need
A sign of life to the land besides
Of nourishing springs for the plants
What wrong is it for the frogs to sing
Croaking forth like angels in applause
Though of cause hiding their faces
To save a fairy who might pass by
Of another episode of a hoax marriage.

Merry it is to all but the farmer
Who in time has to vice up
Of ideas and efforts to control the river
But it never gives a damn
Like a hurricane, it sweeps all
Even the last grains the farmers has
To assure him seldom of a harvest
Poor farmers who controls not the river
To live by the river and dread his visits.

But to mourn or not to mourn
Seems to be an event in time
Of the rivers swelling and losing track
Like the hunter who knows not the skills
To trap a game and know not to untrap it
So is the river, fateful to a drunkard
Who by sober drunkenness masters his way
Though today the river has moved
To carry the drunkard all in a bath
Alas, down the stream we get the corpse.

SPEAK FOR ME

Will you in your zeal speak for me when I speak no more
Will you tell of all that I so want to say
Will you try and be me even when you know it's hard
Will you speak to say no! When they say yes
Will you make sure that all is well when am gone
Will you please say, you will indeed speak for me?

THANK YOU

It has been a while for me to say thank you
In all that I have failed you at over time
I regret the silence when all you wanted was a thank you
For I could never repay for your kindness
For the smile and joy that is in me from you
For the memories though jaded never to ignore
For the hope that in darkness made me sigh
For the dreams that by you would come true
Allow me this one last time before I check out
To say with fondness and humour of life
I have always meant to say thank you.

CASTLE

He calls you his castle
For in awe he adores your might
For the elegance that you are
Standing high in the middle of the city
A reminder of time immortal
You are indeed his castle

In admiration I envy his excitement
To know that it is joy to him knowing you in glory
That nothing can in awe compare
For your place is irrevocable
With applause and jubilation
You are indeed my castle too.

DADDY

It is not too long that I loved to be young
To know that naivety and stupidity would be excused
For in my err I was but indeed a child
To look up for all to decide and take the step
For life indeed must have been easy

Yet with no regret do I regret
To know that with time it all fades away
To listen to the quite nights for daddy's call
For now I am no more a stupid sill child
He expects me to be daddy even when I want to be him

The melancholic intrigue of knowing what is
With love and adoration to smile and laugh
For I admire the way he looks up
To know that there is and always will be hope
For in me she forever confides, I am indeed daddy!

THE END

Breinigsville, PA USA
06 April 2011
259350BV00002B/138/P